# I Used To Be Afraid Of... Dogs

Does this dog look scary to you? It has big jaws and big teeth. Is it angry? Will it bite?

Does your heart pound when you hear dogs bark? Do you run if you see a dog on the street? Dogs can be frightening. They bark, howl, growl, and jump around.

Would you be scared to see these dogs? They look like they are fighting, but they are really playing! If you learn about dogs, you won't be afraid. Most dogs are friendly, even when they are making noise.

I USED to be AFRAID of
DOGS,
but now I know . . .

Newborn dogs are called puppies. They are soft and cuddly. Their eyes are closed at first. They stay next to their mother, drinking her milk.

The puppies grow fast. At four weeks they tumble around, playing with each other. They begin to eat solid food.

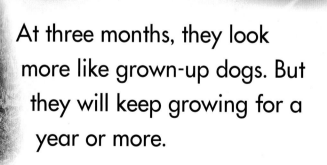

At three months, they look more like grown-up dogs. But they will keep growing for a year or more.

I USED to be AFRAID of DOGS, but now I know . . .

Dogs come in all shapes and sizes. Their fur may be long or short. Their ears may stand up or flop over. Some are solid brown or black. Some have spots. They are all dogs.

Some dogs drool and slobber. Have you seen a dog with its tongue hanging out of its mouth? It is just panting. Panting is how dogs cool off.

I USED to be AFRAID of
DOGS,
but now I know...

A dog can sniff out hundreds of scents that you can't smell. Dogs can even smell things that are buried in the ground! What's that smell? A dog knows!

This dog uses its nose to find missing people. The dog sniffs a piece of clothing to get the person's scent. Then it follows the scent to find the person.

I USED to be AFRAID of DOGS, but now I know . . .

Dogs help people in many ways. They help hunters find birds and other animals. They help farmers herd sheep.

Feeling sad? Call Doctor Dog! Some dogs visit people who are lonely or sick. Just petting and cuddling a dog can help people feel better. Some dogs are guides and helpers for blind and disabled people.

I USED to be AFRAID of DOGS, but now I know . . .

A dog can be your best buddy. If you treat a dog with love and kindness, the dog will love you back.

Dogs love to play and cuddle. And dogs are loyal to their owners. A pet dog is really like a member of the family.

Sometimes dogs bark to warn strangers away. They are protecting their homes. Dogs also bark as a way to communicate, or they'll growl while playing.

Some unfriendly dogs can be dangerous. You can tell when a dog is unfriendly. It holds its tail stiffly. The hair on its back stands up. The dog barks or growls. If you do come across an unfriendly dog, just slowly walk away. Don't run, because the dog may chase you if you do. Try not to scream or stare at the dog. That may make the dog more excited.

I USED to be AFRAID of DOGS, but now I know . . .

Dogs are friends, playmates, and helpers. And most dogs love people. Just leave strange and unfriendly dogs alone, and don't let them scare you.